18160754 9

CW01475557

Pebble® Plus

LET'S LOOK AT COUNTRIES

LET'S LOOK AT
ECUADOR

BY MARY BOONE

raintree
a Capstone company — publishers for children

Raintree is an imprint of Capstone Global Library Limited, a company incorporated in England and Wales having its registered office at 264 Banbury Road, Oxford, OX2 7DY – Registered company number: 6695582

www.raintree.co.uk
myorders@raintree.co.uk

Edited by Jessica Server
Designed by Juliette Peters
Picture research by Jo Miller
Production by Laura Manthe
Originated by Capstone Global Library Ltd
Printed and bound in India

ISBN 978 1 4747 8447 4 (hardback)
ISBN 978 1 4747 8464 1 (paperback)

British Library Cataloguing in Publication Data
A full catalogue record for this book is available from the British Library.

Photo Credits
Alamy: Carlos Mora, 16, Alamy/Kumar Sriskandan, 20-21; Dreamstime: Barbiedohl, 13; Newscom: imageBROKER/Karol Kozlowski, 18-19; Shutterstock: Ammit Jack, 6-7, 9, Atlaspix, 22 (Inset), Don Mammoser, 17, Fotos593, 4-5, JKom, 11, JopsStock, 1, Ksenia Ragozina, Cover Middle, 2-3, 8, Martin Mecnarowski, 22-23, 24, nale, 4 (map), SL-Photography, 15, Uwe Bergwitz, Cover Top, Vaclav Sebek, Cover Bottom, Cover Back

CONTENTS

Where is Ecuador?

Ecuador is in South America.

It is about the same size
as the United Kingdom.
The capital city is Quito.

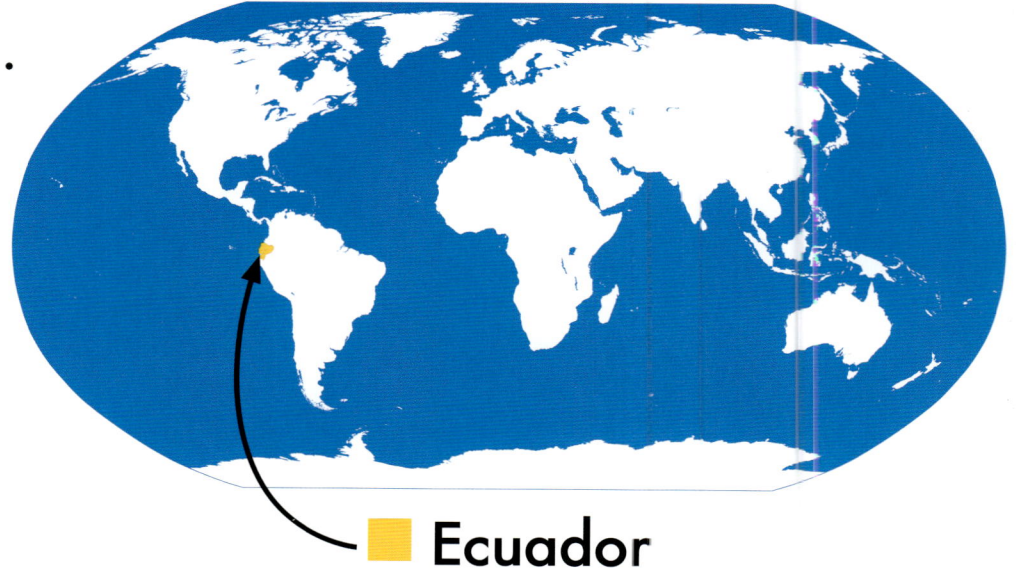

Ecuador

Quito

From beaches to mountains

Ecuador has beaches along the coast. The Galápagos Islands are out in the Pacific ocean. The Andes Mountains are in the centre of Ecuador. Part of the Amazon Rainforest covers the east.

the Andes mountain range

In the wild

Ecuador is home to many kinds of animals. Monkeys live in the rainforest. So do tapirs, birds and snakes. Giant tortoises live on the Galápagos Islands.

woolly monkey

tapir

People

Native Americans have lived in Ecuador for thousands of years. Europeans settled there in the 1500s. Today most people speak Spanish. Native peoples also speak Quechua.

At the table

Llapingachos are common in Ecuador.

They are potato patties with cheese.

People eat them with a fried egg,

avocado and peanut sauce.

llapingachos

Festivals

In June many people celebrate
Inti Raymi. It is the festival
of the sun. People enjoy food,
parades and dancing.

At work

Many people in Ecuador work in the oil business. Some work in tourism. Some are farmers. They grow bananas and coffee beans.

Transport

People use buses and taxis a lot in Ecuador. Boats carry visitors between islands. Trucks are used as buses and taxis in rural areas.

Famous place

The Galápagos Islands are famous. Thousands of people visit them each year. They go to see the many rare plants and animals.

Galápagos tortoise

QUICK ECUADOR FACTS

Ecuador's flag

Name: Ecuador
Capital: Quito
Other major cities: Guayaquil, Cuenca, Santo Domingo
Population: 17 million (November 2018 estimate)
Size: 276,840 sq km (106,888 square miles)
Language: Spanish
Money: US dollar

GLOSSARY

capital   the city in a country where the government is based

famous   known about by many people

patty   a small, flat cake

rainforest   a thick forest where rain falls almost every day

rare   not often seen, found or happening

rural   to do with the countryside

settle   to make a home in a new place

tortoise   a turtle that lives only on land

tourism   guiding or helping tourists

FIND OUT MORE

Books

Ecuador (All Around the World), Joanne Mattern (Pogo Books, 2019)

Galápagos Islands (In Focus), Clive Gifford (Kingfisher, 2018)

South America (Introducing Continents), Chris Oxlade and Anita Ganeri (Raintree, 2018)

Websites

These websites include information about Ecuador and the Galápagos Islands and why the islands are so important.

kids.kiddle.co/Galápagos_Islands

www.bbc.com/bitesize/articles/zk9cxyc

www.natgeokids.com/uk/discover/geography/countries/ng-kids-heads-to-the-galapagos-islands/

COMPREHENSION QUESTIONS

1. What types of jobs do people in Ecuador have?

2. Which animal from Ecuador would you be most excited to see?

3. What do people do to celebrate Inti Raymi?

INDEX